Extreme Survival Handbook

Claire Llewellyn

tangerine
press

an imprint of
■SCHOLASTIC
www.scholastic.com

Author: Claire Llewellyn
Consultant: Dr. Peter Barnes,
The Institute for Outdoor
Learning

A Marshall Edition
Edited and designed by
Marshall Editions Ltd.
74 Shepherd's Bush Green
Shepherd's Bush
London W12 8QE; England
www.marshallpublishing.com

Copyright © 2001 Marshall
Editions Developments Ltd.

an imprint of
SCHOLASTIC
www.scholastic.com

Published by Tangerine Press,
an imprint of Scholastic Inc.;
557 Broadway; New York
NY 10012

10 9 8 7 6 5 4 3 2 1

ISBN 0-439-83668-9

Originated in Leeds, United
Kingdom by Grasmere (Digital
Printing) Ltd.

Scholastic Canada
Markham, Ontario

Scholastic Australia
Gosford, NSW

Scholastic New Zealand
Greenmount, Auckland

Printed and bound in China

CONTENTS

3

READ THIS FIRST:

Most of us like to go off on adventures—hiking in the mountains, sailing on the sea, or flying to another country. But our trips do not always go smoothly: we could meet an avalanche; we could meet a shark; our plane could be forced to crash land.

And you don't have to be an adventurer to meet disaster. Billions of people live in places where there are volcanoes, earthquakes, floods, and hurricanes. Knowing what to do during an emergency can make the difference between life and death. This book prepares you for the worst!

The book is divided into two sections. The first section deals with real emergencies—such as crocodiles, floods, and fire—which we hope will happen only in your imagination. The second section has lots of useful tips such as how to find food, shelter, and water, which could be helpful on hiking trips.

As you go through the book, you'll find a number of pages for you to record your own adventures—real or imaginary.

This book tackles some extreme situations and gives advice on how to cope with them. Never go looking for adventures like these. NEVER put yourself in dangerous situations to test whether our advice really works! Neither the writer nor the publishers can accept any responsibility for any injuries, damage, loss, or prosecutions resulting from the information in this book.

Animal Dangers

SNAKES live all over the world, but especially in warm places such as deserts and rainforests. They are found on the ground, in water, and in the branches of trees.

IF YOU ARE WALKING IN SNAKE COUNTRY...

- Always wear long pants, thick socks, and boots.
- Keep to marked trails.
- Never move rocks or logs with your bare hands.
- Never climb trees that have very thick leaves.
- Never swim in muddy rivers.

IF YOU SEE A SNAKE...

- Stand very still.
- Don't go near it or try to touch it.
- Never try to prod or kill it.
- Back away slowly and give it lots of room. Snakes can strike half their body length in an instant, and some are over 6 ft. (2 m) long.

WHAT TO DO

Python

ATTACK!

IF YOU ARE BITTEN...

- Find a doctor immediately even if you know the snake is not poisonous. Bites can cause infections and allergic reactions.
- If you can't reach a doctor within 30 minutes, wrap a bandage about 3 in. (8 cm) above the bite to slow down the flow of venom. The bandage should be loose enough to slip a finger underneath it.
- Never try to suck out the poison. You could swallow it.
- Never try to cut out the poison. You could start an infection.
- Do not put anything cool, such as ice, on the bite.

HOW TO TREAT A BITE...

Wash the bite with soap and water as soon as you can, cover it with a clean cloth, and keep the bitten area immobilized in a position lower than the heart. This slows down the flow of venom. If you are sprayed in the eyes with venom, wash it out with whatever you have on hand—water, milk, or even urine!

Did you know?

Snakes never eat people. They don't attack because they are hungry. They attack us because they are very frightened or because they mistake us for their usual prey.

CROCODILES and alligators live in the warmer parts of the world. They are found in the slow-moving water of creeks and rivers, in lakes, or in mangrove swamps along the coast.

TRAVELING IN CROCODILE COUNTRY...

- Always keep a sharp lookout for crocodiles both on land and water.
- Never enter water where crocodiles are known to live.
- On boat trips, avoid swamps, bays, and tidal pools—especially at night when crocodiles and alligators are more active. Never put your hands or feet over the side of a boat.
- Always treat crocodiles with respect. They can move faster than you can run.

WHAT TO DO

IF YOU SEE A CROCODILE...

- Never approach a crocodile or alligator. Freeze and slowly back away.
- Never try to feed crocodiles or alligators. You may make them lose their fear of humans.
- Never approach the eggs or babies. The mother will be near enough to hear her young's distress calls. She will certainly attack.

IF YOU ARE ATTACKED...

ATTACK!

- Try to hit the animal on the nose or in the eyes. Use a weapon if you can.
- If the animal is holding any part of your body in its jaws, punch it very hard on the end of its snout. This should make it open its mouth.
- If you are on land, try to get on the animal's back and push down on its neck. This will force its head down.
- Cover its eyes with something. This should calm it down.
- If the animal has you in its jaws, try to keep its mouth clamped shut. This will stop it from shaking and seriously wounding you.

Crocodile

Did you know?

Most crocodiles and alligators rush into the water if they see humans, unless they feel cornered or are defending their nest.

HOW TO TREAT A BITE...

As soon as possible, pour water over the wound for at least five minutes. Then cover the wound with a clean bandage.

Find a doctor as soon as you can, even if you're only bruised and shaken. Crocodiles and alligators carry germs in their mouths, which can start nasty infections.

THERE are over 370 types of sharks, and they live all over the world. Very few sharks are a danger to swimmers. Those sharks that do attack usually live in warm waters.

HOW TO AVOID A SHARK ATTACK...

- Try to swim with other people. Sharks are more likely to attack someone swimming alone.
- Never swim after dusk. Though sharks will attack in the day, they are most active in the evening.
- Never go in the sea if you are bleeding. The smell of blood can attract sharks.
- Never wear a watch or jewelry in the water. They glitter like fish scales.
- Never swim where people are fishing. Dead fish and bait may attract sharks.
- If you are diving or surfing, do not lie on the surface. From below, you may look like a turtle or a seal, or other shark prey.

WHAT TO DO

IF YOU SEE A SHARK...

- Sharks sometimes follow boats. If you see a shark, do not enter the water.
- A shark that allows itself to be seen may simply be curious about you. Try to remain calm.
- If you think that the shark is going to damage your boat, try frightening it away with big actions and loud noises. As a last resort, jab it on the nose with a paddle.
- If you are in the water, get out as quickly and quietly as you can, swim using the breaststroke. Do not shout, splash, or kick wildly in the water. To a shark, you may sound like a wounded animal.

ATTACK!

IF YOU ARE ATTACKED...

- Try to punch or poke the shark hard in its eyes or gills. If you have any equipment in your hands, use it as a weapon.
- Keep on hitting the shark. The animal may decide to give up the attack and look for easier prey.
- If a shark bumps you in the water and then swims away, it may be preparing to attack. Get out of the water as soon as you can.
- If you are wounded, find help and get to a hospital as soon as you can. Shark bites can cause blood loss and infection. The wound will need cleaning, dressing, and maybe stitching.

Did you know?

People kill about 100 million sharks every year. Yet only about 100 people die each year in shark attacks.

White shark

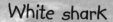

11

BEARS live in the mountains and forests, where they feed on small mammals, fish, and plants. They are shy creatures, but also curious, so if you hike or camp in the forest, there is a slim chance you will see one.

Did you know?
A large bear may stand up to 10 ft. (3 m) high and weigh up to half a ton.

WALKING IN BEAR COUNTRY...

- Stay on marked trails.
- As you walk along, talk loudly, call out, clap your hands, and sing. This will frighten bears away.
- Walk in a group. Never wander off alone.
- Never hike at night, when bears are active.
- Bears can smell food from a long way away. Wrap any food you have and store it in a "bear safe" container. Dispose of trash carefully.
- If you are camping, never eat or keep any food in your tent—not even a bar of chocolate.
- If you come across a dead animal, leave it alone. Look around carefully and move on.

Did you know?
Bears are most dangerous when they are with their cubs or when they are eating a recent kill.

IF YOU MEET A BEAR... **WHAT TO DO**

- Do not make eye contact. Stand still, keep quiet, and then slowly back away. The bear will probably leave you alone.
- Never shout or run away. A bear can run much faster than you can.
- Never stop to take a photo.
- If you are in a car, stay where you are. Do not get out or open the windows.
- Never approach bear cubs. Their mother will be near by and will attack to defend her young.
- Sometimes a bear charges, but is bluffing. If you can, stand your ground, and do not run away.
- Do not climb a tree. Bears can be very good tree climbers and will follow you.

ATTACK!

IF YOU ARE ATTACKED...

- Fall to the ground and roll into a ball with your hands behind your neck. If you are wearing a backpack, leave it on. It will protect you if the bear cuffs you.
- Play dead for as long as you can. The bear will probably leave you alone. If it wanders off, wait for a while, then move away slowly, checking for other bears.
- If a bear attacks you at night in your tent, strike back with anything you can. Aim for the animal's eyes or nose. Make as much noise as you can.
- If you are injured, clean the wound and seek medical help as soon as possible.

WILD CATS, such as the mountain lion (also known as the cougar, panther, or puma) live in forests, grasslands, and mountains. They are shy, but will defend their territory if they feel threatened.

WALKING IN WILD-CAT COUNTRY...

- Do not hike alone, especially after dusk when wild cats are active.
- Make plenty of noise to reduce the chance of surprising a cat.
- Keep a lookout for places where a cat might hide, such as rocks or low-lying bushes.
- Stay close to the adults in your group. Do not walk off alone or straggle behind.
- Carry a good walking stick. It may be useful to frighten a cat.

WHAT TO DO

IF YOU MEET A WILD CAT...

- Never approach a cat. Give it the time and space to escape.
- Stay calm and face the animal, making eye contact. Back away slowly and do not run.
- Pick up younger children. This makes you look bigger and stops them from running away.
- Speak or growl at the cat firmly in a loud voice. This will show it that you are not prey and that you may possibly be a danger.
- If the cat follows, try to appear larger by opening your jacket or raising your arms and waving them slowly.
- Do not crouch down or bend over. This makes you look like four-legged prey!

IF YOU ARE ATTACKED...

ATTACK!

- Without turning your back or bending over, throw branches, stones, or anything you can.
- Fight back aggressively—the wild cat needs to understand that you are not prey and might be a danger to it. Go for the head, aiming for the eyes and mouth in particular. Use anything you can as a weapon—a stick, cap, jacket, or just your bare hands. Protect your neck and throat carefully. This is the area the cat will attack.

Did you know?

When it is angry, a pet cat behaves like a wild cat. It crouches down, flattens its ears, twitches its tail, and growls.

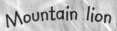
Mountain lion

MANY bees are social insects that live in large groups called colonies. They are usually peaceful creatures, but at times they can become very angry and may attack in swarms.

IF YOU SEE A BEES' NEST...

- Learn to recognize bees' nests. They are brown oval masses attached to tree trunks or branches high above the ground. Some bees nest in the ground. Always keep well away.
- Never bother bees. If you see them building a nest near your home, do not disturb them. Bees will sting to defend their nest, and some are extremely dangerous. Seek help from Pest Control.
- If you are near a nest when a swarm is disturbed, sit still for at least five minutes. When the threat has passed, crawl away slowly and carefully.

ATTACK!

IF YOU ARE ATTACKED...

- Run away at once. Do not swat the bees. This will make them even angrier.
- If possible, seek shelter and get indoors. If there is no shelter, run through the thickest and bushiest foliage you can find. The branches will spring back and confuse the insects.
- Do not jump into a pond, a river, a swimming pool, or any other type of water, because the swarm of bees will most likely be waiting when you surface.

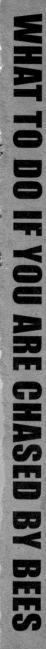

Did you know?

The Brazilian government once had to send soldiers armed with flamethrowers to deal with a bee attack at a school playground.

Most bees swarm in the spring and fall. This is when they start a new nest.

A bees' nest may contain up to 60,000 bees.

Did you know?

Angry bees may chase you for about 460 ft. (140 m)—that's farther than the length of a football field.

WHAT TO DO

IF YOU ARE STUNG...

When a bee stings, it leaves its sting full of poison in your skin. Remove it gently by brushing it with a fingernail or pulling it with tweezers. If you have trouble breathing, get medical help immediately—you may be having an allergic reaction.

17

ANTS including army—or driver—ants and fire ants, can give a nasty sting. Army ants are found in warm, wet rainforests. Fire ants live in South America and the U.S. They all live in large groups called colonies.

WHAT TO DO

IF YOU SEE A COLUMN OF ANTS...

- Get out of its path. Warn other people, if you can.
- Lead any young children away from the area. Help the adults carry any babies in the group.
- Free any animals from ropes or pens. Horses, goats, and chickens could all be killed if they are in the path of driver ants.

ATTACK!

IF YOU ARE ATTACKED...

- If you walk into a colony of ants on the march, keep still, or you will break the trail of scent that the ants are following. If their scent trail is disturbed, the ants will probably run in all directions—perhaps even up your body.
- Do not shake your legs in panic. If you alarm the ants, they can produce a special chemical, which will make the other ants in the colony attack you.
- If the ants actually attack and sting you, run away fast. The quickest way of getting rid of them is by jumping into water, but be sure it is safe to do so. Never put yourself at risk in or near water.

WHAT ANTS DO...

- Army ants form long columns, containing millions of creatures. These creatures then work together as a savage predator.
- They form living bridges over cracks and gaps for other ants to cross.
- They make raids through the forest, killing everything in their path—crickets, spiders, scorpions, snakes, and lizards. They kill about 100,000 insects and other creatures a day.
- Ants sting and bite when they are disturbed. Driver ants have very sharp jaws and could kill any animals that are tied up and unable to run away. Fire ants sting over and over again. The sting causes a burning feeling and leaves white, itchy blisters.

The five animals that I would most like to see...

_____

_____

_____

_____

_____

The five animals that I would least like to meet...

_____

_____

_____

_____

_____

Places I would most like to visit and things I would really like to see...

_____

_____

_____

_____

_____

_____

_____

_____

_____

_____

_____

The time I met a really scary animal...

_____

_____

_____

_____

_____

_____

_____

_____

_____

_____

_____

Natural Dangers

QUICKSAND is soft, wet, sticky sand that is easy to sink in. The ground you walk on is resting on water. Quicksand is found where water and sand or clay are side by side – riverbeds, ocean coasts, prairies, and mountain streams.

BEFORE YOU SET OUT...

- If you know you are going to be walking where there might be quicksand, take a sturdy pole or walking stick with you. This will be useful for testing the ground before you step on it, and if you do get stuck in quicksand, you can use it to help get yourself out safely.
- Places that are well-known for having areas of quicksand usually have warning signs, so watch out for them when you are walking.

IF YOU GET CAUGHT IN QUICKSAND...

- Quickly warn anyone who is behind you, to stop them falling into it, too. You will probably need their help to get out.
- Try to reach firm ground or grab something like a tuft of grass that might help you pull yourself free.
- Take off your backpack and anything else that will weigh you down.

ACTION!

HOW TO AVOID SINKING...

- If you get stuck in quicksand, try to remain calm. Do not panic. Don't thrash around because the more you move, the faster the quicksand will pull you down. Only make slow movements.
- Lean backward and spread out your arms and legs. This should help you float.
- If you have a stick with you, lean across it. Then, move it crosswise under your hips, where it will help to support you as you move.
- Gently push yourself toward firmer ground, taking the shortest route you can.

IF SOMEONE ELSE IS IN QUICKSAND...

- Do not plunge into the quicksand. You will only get trapped yourself.
- Tell the person to stay calm and move slowly.
- Find a long stick or branch. Lay down at the edge of the quicksand and hold out the branch so the person can grab it. Pull the person to safety.

WHAT TO DO

Did you know?

Some quicksand is quicker than others! "Slow" quicksand allows you to take a few steps into it, and still be able to turn around and get out.

HURRICANES are dangerous, swirling storms that bring high seas, huge waves, heavy rains, and terrifying winds. They start over the sea, then head toward land where they can cause a lot of damage.

IF YOU LIVE IN A HURRICANE PRONE AREA...

- Help to make sure your house is sturdy and in good repair.
- Make sure there are plenty of wooden boards, batteries, tools, canned food, water, and a radio in the house at the start of the hurricane season.
- Always listen for hurricane watches and warnings. These are usually given 36 hours in advance.

WHAT TO DO

ACTION!

IF A HURRICANE IS ON THE WAY...

- Help board up the windows and doors.
- If there is a risk of flooding, move valuable things upstairs.
- If you live near the coast or in a mobile home, you will be told to evacuate. Make sure your family allows plenty of time to do this.
- Take your pets with you or lock them inside the house. Leave food and water for them. Pets will not be allowed at evacuation shelters.
- If you are staying at home, prepare to ride out the hurricane in the cellar, a safe room, or a hallway that has no windows. Furnish this area with everything you'll need for 72 hours.

IF YOU ARE RIDING OUT A HURRICANE...

- Stay indoors and stay away from windows and doors. Keep them all tightly shut.
- If the power goes out, use candles and flashlights to light your house. Be sure your parents are lighting and checking on the candles.
- Be prepared for a lot of noise. Hurricane winds can blow up to 150 mph (240 km/h), and last for a long time.
- The middle of a hurricane is a calm spot called the "eye" where the rain and wind die down. The "calm" may last for a few minutes, so do not go outside.
- Listen to a battery-powered radio for weather and evacuation information. Only go outside when you are given the okay that the hurricane is over.

A hurricane moves like a huge spinning top. It is up to 6 mi. (10 km) high and up to 400 mi. (645 km) across.

Did you know?

Hurricanes happen between June and October north of the Equator and between November and March south of the Equator.

MOVEMENTS deep inside the Earth cause earthquakes. During an earthquake the ground shakes violently, roads break up, and buildings and bridges can collapse.

IF YOU LIVE IN AN EARTHQUAKE ZONE...

- Earthquakes happen suddenly and are very difficult to predict. Make sure you know what to do so you are prepared.
- Get an adult to make sure there is a fire extinguisher, plenty of batteries, a supply of canned food, and water in your home.

ACTION!

IF YOU FEEL THE GROUND SHAKE...

- Try to stay calm. Tremors are usually over very quickly.
- If you are at home, stay inside. Take cover under a table, or stand in a doorway, or next to an inside wall.
- Get out of the kitchen and stay away from glass, chimneys, and furniture that might fall.
- If you are in a school or office building, get under a desk. Do not rush for the exits or stairways. Do NOT get into an elevator.
- If you are outside, stay there, but move away from buildings, bridges, and power lines. Stay in an open area until the shaking stops.

Did you know?

Animals sometimes give the first clue that an earthquake is about to happen. Dogs have been known to howl, horses pace, and snakes and rats come out of their holes.

WHAT TO DO

AFTER AN EARTHQUAKE...

- Check yourself for injuries. If you are fine and you know how to do first aid, help anyone who is injured. Beware of broken glass.
- Gas pipes and power lines are often broken in an earthquake and can start a fire. Get an adult to check your home carefully for fires and help put them out with an extinguisher.
- Do not use candles, matches, or open flames in case there is a gas leak.
- Ask an adult to check gas, electricity, and water supplies, but do not turn them on. They should be turned off if there is any damage to pipes or wiring. If you smell gas, leave the building, and get an adult to send for help.
- Be prepared for aftershocks. Listen to the radio for news.
- If you leave the area, do so on foot, taking something to protect your head. Keep away from all buildings and power lines.

AN AVALANCHE is a huge mass of snow that surges down a mountain at high speed. An avalanche is very dangerous because it buries everything in its path—skiers, villages, and roads.

HOW TO AVOID AN AVALANCHE...

- Be aware when an avalanche is likely to occur, especially on steep slopes, after recent heavy snowfalls, and on warm afternoons.
- Always get advice from someone who knows the area before going into the mountains.
- Always follow avalanche warnings.
- Never ski alone or ski the backcountry without a qualified guide. Avoid crossing steep slopes.
- If a group of you are skiing together, always space yourselves out. That way, if some of you are caught in an avalanche, the others can dig you out.
- An avalanche can happen very quickly. Be prepared and know what to do.

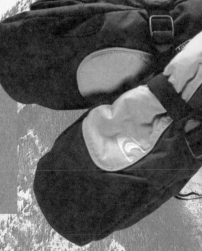

Did you know?

The worst avalanches are 0.6 mi. (1 km) wide and roar down the mountainside at around 225 mph (360 km/h).

WHAT TO DO

IF YOU ARE CAUGHT IN AN AVALANCHE...

- Drop your backpack and other gear.
- Do not attempt to out-ski or out-run the avalanche. It is traveling faster than you. Try to stay upright and move to the edge of the avalanche where the force is less powerful.
- Try to stay on the surface, grab a tree or rock, or thrust yourself upward by kicking.

ACTION!

IF YOU ARE KNOCKED DOWN...

- Let go of your ski poles and try a sort of swimming stroke. If you are falling head first, try breaststroke; if feet first, try backstroke.
- When you come to a stop, curl up into a ball and put your hands in front of your face. Rotate your head to make an air pocket.
- To find out which way is up, spit into your hands and feel which way the saliva runs.
- Try to push one hand to the surface to attract attention, but don't waste energy thrashing about unless you can see daylight.
- Breathe steadily to preserve energy and oxygen. Do not yell until rescuers are near. The snow will stop your voice from carrying.

A FLASH of lightning is a bolt of electricity. It starts inside towering thunderclouds where ice crystals whiz around so fast that the clouds begin to crackle. During a storm, giant sparks surge to the ground.

WHAT TO DO

BE PREPARED...

- Nowhere is completely safe from lightning, so find out which places are safer than others.
- Learn how far away the storm is so you know how much time you have to find shelter (see the opposite page).
- Learn which places to avoid and which objects you should not touch during a storm (see opposite page).

Did you know?

It is a myth that lightning never strikes the same place twice. The Empire State Building in New York, USA, is struck 20–30 times each year.

HOW FAR AWAY IS THE STORM...

To figure out how far away you are from the storm, count the seconds between a flash of lightning and the sound of thunder. Divide the number of seconds by five to learn the distance in miles (by three to discover it in kilometers). If the storm is within 5 mi. (8 km) try to find a safer place immediately.

ACTION!

WHAT TO DO IN A THUNDERSTORM...

- Seek shelter inside a car with the windows up and the doors closed. This is safe because, if the car is struck, the tires will not conduct the electricity.
- Seek shelter inside a building and shut all the doors and windows. Do not stand by the windows.
- Do not use the telephone except for emergencies.
- Avoid wide-open spaces, hilltops, high ridges, and poles. NEVER seek shelter under trees. Lightning usually strikes the highest object.
- Stay away from wire fences or metal objects. Get rid of any metal items you have on you, such as an umbrella or keys.
- If your hair starts to stand on end, it means the air is charged with electricity, and lightning strikes are possible. Drop to your knees and bend over, keeping your head low. Do not lie flat.
- Wait for the storm to pass your area completely. There is a risk of being struck over half an hour after the thunder and rain have stopped.

A tornado is the world's most powerful wind. It is a whirling funnel that destroys everything in its path. There is never much warning before a tornado, so it is important to know what to do.

IF YOU LIVE IN TORNADO COUNTRY

- Prepare an emergency supply kit. You need a first-aid kit, flashlight, batteries, can opener, and a three-day supply of food, water, and medicines.
- Choose a safe place in your home for a tornado shelter. The best place is a small inside room without windows (a bathroom or closet is ideal), a cellar or basement.
- Make sure your family has a plan in case you are separated. You could call an out-of-town friend or relative to say where you are.
- Learn the difference between a tornado watch (when there is a threat of tornadoes) and a tornado warning (when a tornado has been spotted).
- If there is a tornado watch, get ready to move to shelter. You may have only a few minutes.

IF THERE IS A TORNADO WARNING ...

- Always be alert during a thunderstorm. This is when most tornadoes happen.
- Tornadoes can be invisible. A cloud of dust may be the only sign.
- Before a tornado hits, the wind may die down and the air become still.

Did you know?
The winds in a tornado whiz round at over 375 mp. (600 km/h). That's twice as fast as a hurricane!

ACTION!

• IF THERE IS A TORNADO WARNING ...

- If you are outside or in a mobile home, go to an emergency shelter, or an inside hallway or basement in a building with strong foundations.
- Avoid places with large roofs (e.g. theaters, canteens, shopping malls).
- Stay away from windows and glass doors.
- Get under a table or desk and hold on tightly.
- If you are in a car, get out and seek shelter in a building. Never try to out-drive a tornado. The wind can change direction and lift up your car.
- If you can see the tornado, move at right angles away from its path. Lie down in a ditch away from your car and any trees or power lines. Cover your head and neck.

WHAT TO DO

AFTER A TORNADO...

- With your family, see if your neighbors need help. Give them first aid or call for help.
- Use the telephone only for emergency calls.
- Return home when you are sure it is safe. Do not use anything electrical until an adult has checked for gas leaks. If you smell gas, leave the building.
- Do not drink the water if the pipes are damaged.
- Listen to the radio for the latest information.

A BLIZZARD is a winter storm with strong winds, driving snow, and poor visibility. These conditions can be deadly for the unwary traveler.

WHAT TO DO

IF A BLIZZARD STRIKES...

- Seek shelter immediately. Stay indoors if you can.
- If you are outside, don't try to travel. You will have to wait out the blizzard. Dig a trench in the snow and line it with branches to protect you from the wind. Make a roof of branches, too. Mark your shelter in some way (e.g. with ski poles) so that people can see it.
- If the snow is deep, dig yourself a snow hole in a bank. Cold air sinks, so make sure the entrance to your shelter is lower than the place where you sit. Make yourself an airhole and be sure to keep it clear.
- If you are stuck in a car, stay there. If you leave it, you could easily get lost. Hang something bright on the antennae if you can.
- The driver should run the engine ten minutes each hour to keep the car warm, making sure that a window is kept slightly open.
- Clap your hands and keep your legs moving to keep the blood circulating.

Car owners should keep a shovel in their car.

ACTION!

AVOID BEING CAUGHT IN A BLIZZARD...

- At the start of winter, get your family to make sure the car is carrying everything you might need in a blizzard: chains or snow tires, jumper cables, a bag of sand, a shovel for digging out, a windshield scraper, a tow rope, flashlights, blankets, snacks that won't go stale, extra clothing, and a bright cloth to attract attention. A cell phone is useful, too.
- Always listen for weather warnings before you go on any journey.
- When you do go out, always dress warmly.

WHEN THE BLIZZARD IS OVER...

- Be careful if you are digging in heavy snow not to overtire yourself. Cold can be a deadly enemy.
- If you are at home, help the adults check on your neighbors to see that they have enough heat, water, and food.

Did you know?

In 1978, a truck driver spent six days in his truck after being buried in a snowdrift. He survived by eating snow and huddling beneath a blanket.

37

A DESERT gets less than 10 in. (25 cm) of rain a year. It is a dry and very harsh environment. In most deserts, the days are scorching hot and the nights are very cold.

IF YOU ENTER A DESERT...

- Be prepared. Get your parents or guardians to pack the car very carefully with spare gas, spare parts, good maps, and a signaling tool. Take plenty of water. Each person needs at least 1 gal. (4 l) a day.
- Always tell people where you are going and when you plan to return. They can then search for you if you fail to arrive.

HOW TO MAKE A SHELTER...

- Make use of the car or any natural shelter. If you have to build a shelter, wait until it is cool.
- Make shade by building a low "wall" with rocks or branches, and digging a deep trench on the shady side. Or stretch a double layer of cloth over piles of rocks, hold it down with stones, and get underneath. Find somewhere off the ground to rest.

Did you know?
In the desert, a mirror is a good signaling tool. The sun and the open country allow the signal to be seen in all directions.

WHAT TO DO

WHEN YOU ARE IN THE DESERT...

- Travel at night or early morning when it is cooler.
- Stay fully clothed during the day. Clothes protect you from the sun and cut down on water loss.
- Protect your eyes with sunglasses. If you don't have any, rub dirt or ash under your eyes to help cut down on glare.
- Always protect your head. If you don't have a hat, make a covering from leaves or cloth.
- Do not ration water. Drink as much as you need.
- Avoid exercise or work, and have plenty of rest and water; otherwise, you could get heatstroke.
- If the car breaks down, stay by it. This makes it easier to find you.

ACTION!

HOW TO FIND WATER...

- Put a large plastic bag over a cactus or other plant in the sun. Blow up the bag and then tie it closed. In time, water will collect in the bag.
- In the early morning, collect dew from the surface of objects (try metal, leaves, stones) with a cloth and squeeze it into a container.
- Look for signs of water, such as fresh vegetation and flocks of birds.
- Look for signs of an underground well, such as old campsites and crisscrossing paths.
- Cut open cactus stems and chew (but don't swallow) the flesh. It contains valuable juices.
- If you are short of water, do not eat; the body uses water for digestion.

IT IS much more difficult to survive at sea than on dry land. If you go to sea, be prepared for emergencies by taking food supplies and navigation and signaling equipment with you.

ACTION!

IF YOU GO TO SEA...

- Always wear a lifejacket or other buoyancy aid. This will greatly improve your chances of survival.
- Learn to swim. This is useful whether you are at sea or not. Being able to swim will make you feel more confident.
- Make sure an adult packs the following essential items: first aid kit, navigation and signaling equipment, drinking water, dry clothes and blankets, canned food, fishing gear, a flashlight, and batteries.

Dried fruit provides energy and vitamins.

Pack canned food with ring-pulls.

WHAT TO DO

IF YOU ARE IN THE WATER...

- Hold onto anything that will float. Grab as much material as you can. It may be useful to you.
- If you don't have a lifejacket, a pair of pants can keep you afloat. Tie the legs together at the ankles. Blow the pants full of air, put them over your head so there is a leg on either side of you, and hold the waistband tight to your stomach.
- In the water, your body loses heat quickly. Get out as soon as you can.

IF YOU ARE ON A LIFEBOAT...

- Stay on a boat for as long as possible. If you must get into a lifeboat, take whatever supplies you can, especially water and canned foods.
- Stay near the place where your boat (or plane) went down. Rescuers will be looking for you there.
- Try to make a canopy to protect you from the sun, wind, and rain. Keep yourself fully clothed.
- Drink water as you need it. Never drink saltwater or urine. If you are short on water, do not eat.
- Keep a lookout for clouds and be ready to catch rain. Collect it in shoes, bags, and plastic sheets.
- Make a fishing line from twisted thread. Add a fishhook, or make one from wire or wood.
- Fish day and night at different depths. It is safe to eat raw fish.
- Use a mirror or flares to signal to any passing boat or plane.

Did you know?

Raw seabirds are perfectly safe to eat, though they do taste very fishy. Their feathers can be used to make earmuffs or a cap.

A BEACH is safer than the sea, and a much easier to place to survive. Most shorelines offer a supply of fresh water, food, and materials to build a shelter.

WHAT TO EAT...

- There is plenty of food along the shore, so gather shellfish from rocks, making sure that they are alive and healthy. Boil or steam them for at least five minutes.
- Only ever eat foods that you know are safe.
- Look for fish under rocks and in sandy pools.
- The best food plant is the palm tree, which has fruit, sweet sap, tender buds, and starchy stems. Other good foods include seaweed, bamboo shoots, sugar cane, roots, fruit, and nuts.

ACTION!

HOW TO FIND FRESH WATER...

- Look for a fresh stream emptying into the sea.
- Dig a well above the high-tide line, in a dip at the back of the beach. Dig down for at least 3 ft. (1 m), and you will probably find water. It may look nasty, but after boiling, it is safe to drink.
- Unripe (green) coconuts are a good source of water. Cut the nut with a knife or beat it against a rock to open it.

HOW TO BUILD A SHELTER...

- Choose a place out of the wind, well above the high-tide line, and near food and water.
- Build a lean-to frame with branches, and thatch it with fronds and leaves. You can make a useful twine or string from plant fibers.
- You may decide to seek shelter in a cave. Build your fire at the back, so the smoke will rise up and drift out of the cave.
- Make a comfortable bed with palm fronds and other vegetation.

Did you know?
A coconut contains about half a pint (250 ml) of water.

MOVING AROUND...

- Always wear footwear to avoid wounds or stings. You can make shoes from leaves and twine.
- Always observe the tides before exploring other beaches. Travel at low tide and not during the heat of the day.

HOW TO SIGNAL FOR HELP...

- A fire can be seen from a long way away. Place green plants on top of your fire to make a lot of smoke.
- Write a message on the beach. Display your lifeboat, if it is brightly-colored.
- Use a mirror to flash signals to rescuers at sea or in the air.

WHAT TO DO

DURING a long period of heavy rain, streams and rivers swell and rise. They may rise slowly or very quickly, causing floods that can strike with devastating speed.

IF YOU LIVE IN A FLOOD PRONE AREA...

- Listen for flood warnings, especially in the spring. Take them seriously. Always be ready to leave your home.
- Remember that flash floods are not easy to predict. If it is raining heavily, stay away from streams or dry riverbeds. Watch for rising water levels.
- Be prepared with plenty of sandbags. These can keep the water out of your home.
- Keep a supply of canned food that does not require cooking.
- Decide, on a safe route to the nearest high ground, and move there as soon as possible.

WHAT TO DO

IF THE RIVER IS RISING...

- If the river is rising slowly, help to move animals, vehicles, and other important things to higher ground. Avoid low-lying areas that are likely to flood.
- Help lay a wall of sandbags around your home, sealing any places where water could enter.
- Help fill baths, sinks, and other containers with fresh water. After a flood, supplies of drinking water can be contaminated.
- Move any valuables upstairs.

ACTION!

IF YOU HAVE TO LEAVE HOME...

- Listen to the radio for news and weather information.
- If you hear a flash flood warning, get out fast—every second counts.
- Never go in a car through a flooded road. Just 2 ft. (60 cm) of water can carry away a car.
- Never cross a flowing stream if the water is above your knees. Never cross a dry riverbed in a flashflood area.
- Never try to cross water in the dark.
- If you find yourself swept up in a flood, try to grab any floating material and make your way slowly to safe ground.

WHAT TO DO

AFTER THE FLOOD...

- When you return to your home, do not use the lights; the wiring needs to be checked. Use flashlights instead.
- Do not drink tap water until you know it is safe or you have boiled it for at least ten minutes.
- Throw away any food or medicines that have come into contact with flood water.

Did you know?
Flooding takes more lives and destroys more property than any other kind of disaster.

FOREST and brush fires start easily when the weather is hot and plants are very dry. In a strong breeze, these fires spread quickly and are a great threat to people and animals.

IF A FIRE STARTS CLOSE TO YOU...

- Try, with an adult, to smother it immediately with a sleeping bag or beat it out with a coat. If you cannot put it out, notify the forest service or fire department right away.

WHAT TO DO

IF YOU ARE AT HOME...

- Listen to the radio for warnings.
  Always follow the fire department's advice.
- Be prepared to leave the area quickly. Make sure that your family knows the escape plan.
- If you have time, wet your house with a garden hose. This will keep the sparks from setting fire to it easily.

ACTION!

IF YOU ARE IN THE WOODS OR BRUSH...

- Be alert: you can often smell a fire before you see it. Look for animals acting nervous.
- Think about the wind direction. If the wind is blowing toward the fire, move toward the wind.
- If the wind is behind the fire, the flames will move very fast. Do not try to outrun it.
- Look for a road, a stream, or a natural break in the trees that would offer little fuel for the fire. Stay there until the fire has passed.
- If you can, wet your clothing. Then put a damp jacket over your head.

A forest fire can burn an area the size of 400 soccer fields in half an hour.

Did you know?

Old campfires can start a fire. When you put out a campfire, spread out the embers. Pour water over the whole area, allowing it to soak into the ground. Then, top it with sand or dirt.

ONE of the most challenging places on Earth is a frozen wilderness, or even high mountains. The extreme cold and biting winds make it difficult to survive in these places.

TRAVEL IN THE FROZEN WILDERNESS...

- Always tell people where you are going and when you plan to return. Then they will know where to search for you, if you get lost.
- Be prepared. Make sure your parents or guardians pack the car with plenty of fuel, spare parts, signaling and navigation equipment, tools to build a shelter, and matches or another device to make a fire.
- Wear a warm hat, several layers of light, warm clothing, a wind-resistant, waterproof jacket, a couple of pairs of warm socks, and a good pair of waterproof boots. The layers of clothing hold warm air and insulate the body; the jacket keeps out the cold.

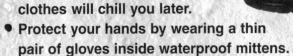

- Unzip or remove a layer of clothes whenever you feel warm. Damp, sweaty clothes will chill you later.
- Protect your hands by wearing a thin pair of gloves inside waterproof mittens.
- Tinted goggles protect against the glare and keep snow and ice out of your eyes.
- A warm, waterproof sleeping bag will stop you from freezing at night.

ACTION!

HOW TO MAKE A SHELTER...

- Build a small shelter, out of the wind, in a place where the snow will not drift. It could be a lean-to shelter, a snow trench, snow cave, or a natural shelter such as a tree hollow, or a rocky cave.
- Lay tree branches on the floor of your shelter to insulate you from the ground.
- Build a fire with dry moss, birch twigs, and larger branches. You may need a windbreak to keep your fire going.
- A wall of branches or stones on the opposite side of your fire will reflect heat back into your shelter.

WHAT TO DO

WHAT TO EAT AND DRINK...

- Melt snow and ice over a fire and strain the water through layers of cloth. Boil it before drinking.
- In the summer months, look for birds' eggs, berries, and lichens (the tiny plants that grow over rocks and tree trunks). Fish for trout and salmon in streams and lakes.
- In winter, catch fish through a hole in the ice. Cut holes about 1 ft. (30 cm) across. Tie hooked and baited lines to sticks, and lay them across the holes.

Did you know?

A naked person exposed to -45°F (7°C) and 30 mph (48 km/h) winds—common conditions in the Arctic—would survive for about 15 minutes.

The worst weather
I have ever seen

_____

_____

_____

_____

_____

_____

_____

_____

_____

_____

_____

_____

What I would do on a desert island

_____

_____

_____

_____

_____

_____

_____

_____

_____

_____

_____

_____

What I would do if there was an earthquake

_____

_____

_____

_____

_____

_____

_____

_____

_____

_____

_____

Human
Hazards

THE MOST important thing to do, if your car begins to sink in water, is to try hard not to panic. Panic makes people forget the simplest things and sometimes costs them their lives.

WHAT TO DO

BEFORE YOUR CAR HITS THE WATER...

- Open your windows as wide as they will go. If you are alone, open as many windows as you can. If there are other people in the car, get them to open their windows.
- REMEMBER that electric windows will not work once the car is under water, so it is very important to open as many of the car windows as possible before you enter the water.

Did you know?
No-one should ever drive a car over a frozen lake or pond, even if they think it's safe. People have often ended up in the water when their car broke through the ice.

BE PREPARED

WHEN YOUR CAR IS IN THE WATER...

- Press the button that releases your seatbelt.
- Get out as soon as you can while the car is still floating. You may have less than a minute.
- You won't be able to open the car doors because the water will be pushing too hard against them. Use a window instead.
- It may be hard to get out of the window while water is rushing in. You may need to wait until the car has filled with water. Take a deep breath and swim out of the car.
- If you can't open the window, find something hard and sharp to break the glass. A screwdriver or a hammer would do the job, but use your foot if you have to.
- Remember that the windshield and back window are harder to break because they are made of tempered glass.

WHAT TO DO

IF YOU CAN'T GET OUT OF THE CAR...

- Try to stay calm. If the car tips or turns upside down, hold onto the steering wheel or a door handle to keep yourself in place.
- When the water level reaches your chin, take a deep breath. By now, you should be able to open a door (the water won't be pushing so hard against it). Get out as quickly as possible and swim to the surface.

HUGE crowds gather at street carnivals, sports events, concerts, and festivals. These events can be a lot of fun, but could lead to a dangerous crush.

WHAT CAUSES CROWD CRUSH...

- Crowd crush occurs when hundreds of people are trying to get to the same place at the same time – for example, into a sports complex or stadium to try to get a good spot to watch the event.
- People rushing to escape from a fire or other danger can cause a crush. They panic and bump into one other and end up moving more slowly.
- Doorways and stairways get blocked when lots of people are trying to use them. The crowd behind starts to push, causing a surge of bodies against the people in front.
- People sometimes get knocked down and trampled in the rush and panic. This is obviously very dangerous for them and prevents others from getting out.

BE PREPARED

HOW TO AVOID A CROWD CRUSH...

- Before going to a big public event, plan where you are going to stand. Some places will be less crowded and easier to leave than others.
- Think carefully before buying tickets for any event that has no seat reservations. Without proper controls, they can be dangerous.
- When you are buying tickets, always choose to sit rather than stand.
- If you are standing, stay near the edge of the crowd and plan what you would do in the event of a crush.

IF YOU ARE IN A CROWD CRUSH...

- If you feel a crush building, move to the edge of the crowd as soon as possible. The push will not be as hard.
- Try to stay calm. It will help you to find a way out. Stay alert, looking around for possible escape routes.
- If you are inside a building, look around carefully. Remember that exit signs may be hard to see.

WHAT TO DO

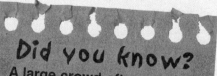

Did you know?
A large crowd often acts like a herd. People are so busy following one another that they overlook safe ways out.

SURPRISINGLY, it is quite possible to survive a plane crash. In all but a very few plane accidents, some or all of the passengers survive. As usual, it helps to be well prepared and to stay calm.

BE PREPARED

ON THE FLIGHT...

- Always listen to the safety talk at the beginning of every flight. Bear in mind that every kind of plane is different.
- Read the passenger safety card as the talk is taking place. Read it again before landing.
- In your mind, plan the actions you would need to take in an emergency. Look to see where your nearest two exits are, and count the number of seat rows to them. You may have to leave the plane in smoke or darkness.
- Look at the emergency hatches and see how they open. If you don't understand the instructions, ask a member of the cabin crew to explain them.
- In the air, always keep your seatbelt fastened. The belt should fit low and snugly across your hips.
- Wear comfortable clothes made of natural fabrics, such as cotton or wool. These will not melt in a fire. Long sleeves and pants will protect your arms and legs.

WHAT TO DO

IF THERE IS AN EMERGENCY LANDING...

- Always follow the instructions of the cabin crew.
- Prepare for an emergency landing by pulling your seatbelt as tight as you can. Bend forward with your hands on your head.
- If you are over water, put on your life vest, which is usually under your seat. Do not inflate it until you have left the plane.
- After landing, try to stay calm and make your way to the exit. Leave all your bags behind.
- Move away from the smoke or fire. If possible, place a wet paper towel or handkerchief over your nose and mouth.
- If you need to use an emergency slide, jump onto it feet first with your arms across your chest. Take your shoes off first.

Did you know?
In the USA, an emergency airplane evacuation takes place every 11 days.

WHAT TO DO

WHEN YOU ARE OUTSIDE THE PLANE...

- Move away from the aircraft: it may catch fire. Never go back inside a burning plane.
- Wait for the emergency vehicles and if you can, help others who need it.

THE KEY to getting out of a burning building is to know the best escape routes. Be prepared, so you are able to react quickly.

BE PREPARED

BE READY FOR A FIRE...

- Make sure there is a fire extinguisher in your house, so a small fire can be put out quickly.
- Have a smoke alarm on every floor of the house.
- Make a good escape plan. You need to have two ways to get out of every room.
- Agree on a meeting place where the family can gather. This way everyone will know that every family member is safe.

WHAT TO DO

IF THERE IS A FIRE...

- As soon as you hear a smoke alarm, get out fast. Do not waste time saving your belongings.
- Take the safest exit route, avoiding smoke where possible.
- If you must go through smoke, crawl along the ground, where the air is easier to breathe. Cover your mouth and nose with a damp cloth.
- If you come to a closed door, put your hand on it. Never open a door that is hot to the touch. If the door is cool, open it slowly with your shoulder against it. If heat and smoke come out, slam it shut immediately.

ONCE YOU ARE OUTSIDE...
- Call the fire department from a neighbor's house.
- Never go back into a burning building.
  Wait for the fire department to arrive.

IF YOU ARE IN A PUBLIC BUILDING...
- Leave quickly, as soon as you hear the
  smoke alarm, closing all doors behind you.
  Never use the elevators.
- If you cannot escape safely, try to go to a
  room with a window and a telephone.
- Use tape, or anything else, to seal air vents
  and cracks around the door.
- Call the fire department and tell them where
  you are, even if you can see firefighters outside.
  Wave something at the window to show them
  your position.
- Be patient. Rescuing people from a building
  may take several hours.

Did you know?
Smoke contains poisonous
gases, which can be deadly.
Most deaths in house fires
are caused by breathing
in smoke.

ABANDONING a ship should be done as orderly as possible, but you need to stay calm, think clearly, and move fast.

BE PREPARED

ON BOARD THE SHIP...

- Always take part in safety drills. This will prepare you for a real emergency.
- Read the safety notices on display. These explain the emergency signals, how to put on a lifejacket, and where the lifejackets and lifeboats are kept.
- Take note of the signs in passageways and stairways that direct you to the lifeboats.

WHAT TO DO

IF THERE IS AN EMERGENCY...

- React quickly. Listen for any safety announcements, and follow them.
- If you are below deck, work your way upstairs as quickly as possible.
- If the ship is listing (leaning over), stay as high as you can. Hold onto pipework or some other fixture, and make your way to the deck.
- Try not to panic and stay alert. Breathing deeply will help you keep calm.

IF YOU HAVE TO ABANDON SHIP...

- If there is time, put on as much warm clothing as possible to cover every part of your body. Securely fasten your lifejacket.
- If you are going to be seasick, take a tablet. Being sick could affect your chances of surviving.
- Get into a lifeboat either on deck or from a ladder or rope. Avoid entering the water, if possible.
- If you are in the water, swim to a nearby lifeboat, to another survivor, or a floating object you can lean on. Otherwise, keep as still as you can to prevent losing body heat.
- If you have a whistle on your lifejacket, use it to attract attention. Get out of the water as soon as possible.

Lifejacket

Did you know?
Lifeboats should always stay near a sinking ship. There have been cases when the ship did not sink, and passengers were able to reboard it.

What I would do if
I was on a sinking ship

_____

_____

_____

_____

_____

_____

_____

_____

_____

_____

_____

My family's fire safety plan

_____

_____

_____

_____

_____

_____

_____

_____

_____

_____

_____

My best trip ever

_____

_____

_____

_____

_____

What I saw and what I brought back

_____

_____

_____

_____

_____

_____

Basic
Survival
Skills

BEFORE you set out, it's important to make sure that you're in good condition for the trip. Make your preparations carefully. Taking the right clothes and equipment could save your life!

Personal check-up

- A few months before you leave, get yourself in good condition with regular exercise.
- Check whether you need any vaccinations or medication for the countries you are planning to visit. Arrange this well ahead of time.
- If you wear glasses or contact lenses, consider taking another pair.
- If you have a medical condition, make sure you take plenty of your usual medication.

Packing your clothes

Think carefully about what you pack. Pack what you need for the climate. If you are going somewhere hot, take loose-fitting cotton clothing, and a hat. If you are going somewhere it can get cold, pack a warm hat, gloves, socks, boots, loose-fitting clothes, and a windproof, outer layer.

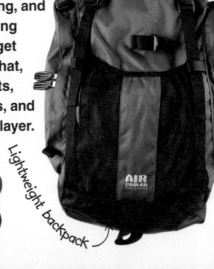

Lightweight backpack

Socks

Packing your essentials

As well as clothes, you'll need to pack a few pieces of basic equipment. These will make life more comfortable and might help you in an emergency. A first-aid kit, matches (with an adult's permission), a small flashlight, and knife are essential equipment.

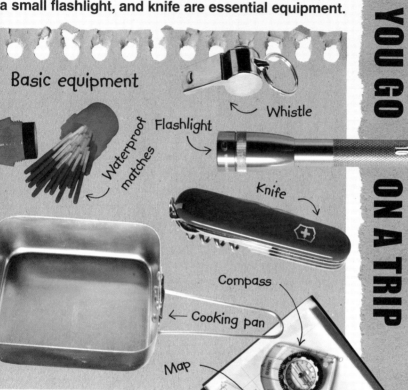

Basic equipment

Whistle

Flashlight

Waterproof matches

Knife

Compass

Cooking pan

Map

Don't forget!

Before you disappear into the wilderness, make sure you tell someone where you are going, and when you plan to return. If something goes wrong, they can send out a search party.

IT IS important to know how to find your way and know where you are. Reading a map and using a compass are useful skills. There are other ways of finding direction, such as using the Sun and stars.

Using a Map

A map is a drawing of the land from a bird's-eye view. You can usually find your position on a map by locating a bridge, a river, or any other nearby landmark. The grid lines on the map help you calculate distances and find your exact position.

Using the stars

On clear nights, you can use two famous star patterns to find your direction. The two end stars on the "bowl" of the Big Dipper constellation in the Northern Hemisphere point toward the bright North Star. North is below this star on the horizon.

In the Southern Hemisphere, find the Southern Cross constellation and draw an imaginary cross to join the four stars. Follow the longer line down to the horizon. This points you toward the South. Visit an observatory to find out more.

Northern Hemisphere   Southern Hemisphere

Using your watch to find your direction

This works best when the Sun is not directly overhead.

In the Northern Hemisphere

Point the hour hand toward the Sun. Imagine a line halfway between the hour hand and 12 o'clock. This line points to the South.

In the Southern Hemisphere

Point the 12 o'clock mark toward the Sun. Imagine a line halfway between this mark and the hour hand. This line points to the North.

South

Direction of Sun

Direction of Sun

North

Using a compass

A compass has a magnetic needle that always points to the Earth's magnetic north. By changing the direction of the compass, you will be able to take a bearing—the exact direction that you should follow. It takes time and practice to use a compass, but it is something you should learn before you travel in the wild. The leader of any Scout or Guide group will be able to help you.

Compass

A GOOD pocketknife is an essential part of your equipment and will help you to perform all sorts of useful tasks. Never abuse your knife. Keep it in good shape and only use it when an adult is present.

Some pocketknives have a single blade, others have a selection of blades and tools.

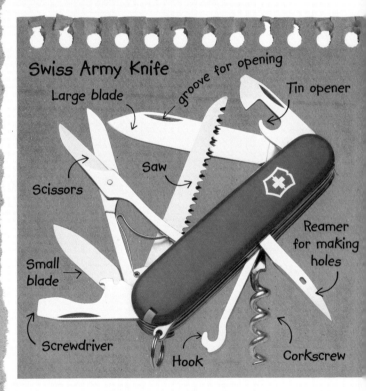

Swiss Army Knife

groove for opening

Large blade

Tin opener

Saw

Scissors

Reamer for making holes

Small blade

Screwdriver

Hook

Corkscrew

Working with a knife

Always cut away from you, if the pocketknife slips, you won't cut yourself. Do not expect too much of your knife. It is easier to cut thin strips of wood rather than large chunks. When you have finished with your knife, clean it, and put it back in your kit. Then, you will always know where it is.

How to sharpen your knife

- A dull knife is dangerous and not very useful for cutting. Use a sharpening stone to keep it sharp.
- Wet the stone slightly with a little spit.
- Lay the sharp edge of the blade against the stone.
- Stroke both sides of the blade against the stone back and forth in a sweeping motion until the edge is sharp. Be sure to ask an adult to help you.
- Now wipe the blade up and down against the inside of a leather belt. This smooths and firms the edge.

Safety tip!

To open a pocketknife put your thumbnail in the groove on the blunt side of the knife and pull out the blade as far as it will go. To close it, place your fingers against the blunt side and gently push it in.

A sharp knife is invaluable for preparing camp food. Wash it before and after use.

HUMANS cannot survive long without water. Fortunately, there are many places in the wild where you can find water. Purify any water you collect, to make it safe to drink.

Where to find water

- Fresh water flows into streams and rivers. These flow along the base of valleys.
- Rain is a good source of clean water. Collect it in a water collector (see opposite page).
- The leaves of fresh, green plants give off water, which you can collect in a bag (see page 39).
- Some plants hold water in their leaves, or carry it in their roots and stems (see page 39).
- Watch wild animals: they might lead you to water.
- Collect dew from cold surfaces in the early morning (see page 39).
- Never wait until you have run out of water before finding some more.

A hiker drinking fresh river water.

Purifying water

1. Water collected from the wild contains germs that could make you ill. Always purify water before drinking it.
2. First, filter your water by pouring it through a clean sock or nylon. Line the sock with a handkerchief or a handful of fine sand.
3. Boil the filtered water for five minutes.
4. When it is cool, store the water in a clean container and keep it in the shade.

Making a water collector

1. Spread out a waterproof sheet on the ground.
2. Peg the sheet with twigs, making sure it is stretched out just above the ground.
3. Put rocks in the middle of the sheet near the edge and place a container near to them.

Rainwater will collect on the sheet, and run into the container.

Container to collect water

Waterproof sheet

How much water?

Our bodies lose water all the time and much more when it is hot, or when we are working hard. In a cool climate, we need to drink 4-5 pints (2-3 liters) a day. In a hot climate, we need twice as much water to prevent dehydration. Dehydration is dangerous and can lead to death.

A CAMPFIRE provides you with heat and light. You can use it to cook your food, purify your water, drive away insects, and dry wet clothes. Learn how to make a fire before you travel in the wild.

Looking for fuel

Look around for the driest kindling and fuel you can find. Gather all the fuel you're likely to need before you light your fire.

What you need to build a fire

Tinder: this catches fire easily

Dead moss   Dead leaves   Strips of bark

Kindling: this gets the fire burning faster

Plenty of fine dry twigs

Main fuel: this keeps the fire burning

Short sticks about as thick as your thumb

How to make a fire

1. Choose a good spot for the fire, well away from bushes, undergrowth, or hanging trees. Lay some main fuel on the ground to make a platform.
2. Place a bundle of tinder on the platform and arrange two handfuls of kindling on top.
3. Place main fuel around the kindling, making a tipi shape. Then light the tinder.

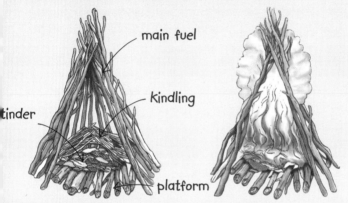

main fuel

kindling

tinder

platform

Making an all-night fire

It's great to sleep next to a glowing fire when you are camping.

- Arrange the embers of your campfire into a long, narrow line.
- Find three long logs about 6 in. (15 cm) across.
- Place one on each side of the embers. Fill the gap between them with kindling. Put the third log on top of the burning kindling.

No scorch marks

Always build a fire on bare earth or some other place where it won't leave ugly scorch marks. In grassy places, cut away a square of grass and replace it when you leave.

- Build a log or stone "wall" on the far side of the fire to reflect heat back into your shelter.

YOU will probably take food on your trip. But, in an emergency, it is useful to know how to find food in the wild. There is a lot of food you can eat, but do not try anything you don't know. It may be poisonous.

Different foods

You'll find different foods in different places: it all depends on the habitat, climate, and season. For example, you'll find seaweed, crabs, shrimp, and shellfish on the seashore; water beetles, waterlily tubers, and eels in rivers; berries and nuts in forests and in the mountains; burdock, nettles, and sorrel in meadows and woods; and insects, snails, and worms almost everywhere!

Wild foods

Whirligig beetle

Edible crab

Burdock

Cloudberries

Recognizing plants

There are thousands of plants that are safe to eat, but it takes time and experience to learn them. Get ready for your trip by finding out what edible plants grow in the area you are traveling in: coconuts and plantains in tropical countries, for example, or cranberries, roots, and lichens in high mountains.

Warning!

Only eat foods that you recognize and know to be safe. If you are not sure, do not eat them.

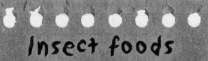

Insect foods

Grasshoppers, termites, butterflies, bees... there are thousands of different kinds of insect. Most of them (and their grubs) are safe and nourishing to eat. Always boil or fry them first.

Notch for fishing line →

Tree branch →

→ Hook

How to make a fishing line

You have a good chance of catching a meal in a stream if you know how to make a simple line.

1. Make the fishing line from soaked, braided plant stems or lengths of twisted thread or twine.
2. Make the hook by cutting a branch about 1 in. (2.5 cm) long with another branch attached to it.
3. Using your knife, shave the attached branch to form a hook. Cut a notch around the other end.
4. Tie your fishing line tight around the notch.
5. Put live bait (insects, grubs, worms) on the hook.

OUT in the wild, without refrigeration, fresh foods go bad quickly, and become breeding grounds for germs. Always cook and eat fresh food quickly, and keep all stored food covered.

Keeping food safe

- Eat all food while it is still very fresh. Meat, seafood, and fish quickly spoil, becoming dangerous to eat.
- Preserve extra meat or fish by drying it. Cut it into thin strips and lay them about 3 ft. (1 m) above a smoky fire until they are dry and brittle.
- Dry fruits by slicing them into thin pieces and putting them in the sun.

Hanging food supply

Storing your food in a hanging net helps to protect it from flies. This is very important in the tropics, where flies can carry disease. Make a "sack" out of fine-mesh net to put around a plate of food. Tie the net together at the top with rope and hang the larder from the branch of a shady tree.

Keeping cool!

In hot weather, keep drinks cool by putting them in a bowl of cold water, or place them in a cool stream, attached to the bank by a rope.

Different ways to cook food

Food can be cooked over a fire on a tripod grill, or on heated stones. Ask an adult for help and be careful not to burn yourself. Dig out a small trench to make a fire. Once it has burned down to a thick bed of hot embers, you can put a grill over the embers or place some foods (e.g. potatoes) directly on them.

Tripod grill

Hot embers

Cooking over a fire:

1. Find a long green stick no thicker than a pencil. Sharpen it at one end.
2. Push small pieces of meat, vegetables, or fish on the stick.
3. Place your stick over the fire until the food is cooked, or put it on a tripod grill to cook over the hot embers.

Cooking on hot stones:

1. Make a bed of large, flat stones.
2. Put tinder and kindling on the top and let it burn for half an hour.
3. Brush away the ashes carefully.
4. Cook your food on the hot rocks. You can wrap the food in leaves or grass (or foil if you have some) to keep the ashes off.

Hot rocks

KNOWING how to build a simple shelter is a very useful skill. A small shelter traps heat and keeps out the worst of the weather. In emergencies, a shelter can help you survive!

Where to build a shelter

- Look for any natural shelter from the weather, such as a cave, a hill, a large rock, a clump of bushes, or a large, spreading tree.
- Look for flat ground. Check that it is dry and unlikely to flood. Avoid hollows in the ground: they could fill with rain.
- Build your shelter away from the wind.

How to build a shelter

1. Make a strong triangular frame by tying one long, and two short branches together. Make sure the frame is large enough for you to lie in.
2. Line the walls of the shelter with short branches.
3. Cover the walls with a 2 ft. (60 cm) layer of leaves, moss, and grass. Cover with a layer of brush (branches and twigs).

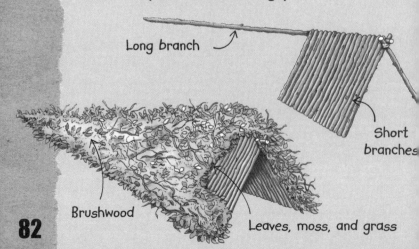

Long branch

Short branches

Brushwood

Leaves, moss, and grass

Finding useful materials

Make your shelter with whatever materials you have on hand: a lifeboat, parachute, stones, rocks, branches, and leaves. Tie branches together with a natural string, made from plant fibers braided together.

A longer stay

If you plan to stay in your shelter for several nights, make sure you build it near food, a place for fire, and water.

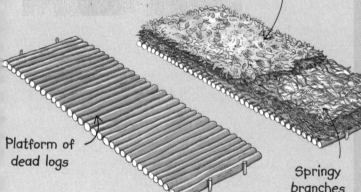

Soft top layer

Platform of dead logs

Springy branches

How to make a bed

Enjoy a good night's sleep on this comfortable bed. It takes just an hour to make.

1. Look for dead logs about 3 ft. (1 m) long and 2 in. (5 cm) across. Lay them on the ground to make a platform. Drive pegs into the ground at each end to stop the logs from slipping.

2. Put a 2 ft. (60 cm) layer of springy branches on top of the logs.

3. Now, cover your "mattress" with softer materials, such as young branches and leaves.

WHEN you enter the wilderness, you are entering the world of animals. Most animals, unless they are injured or hungry, will stay away from humans. We should try to stay away from them too.

Avoiding animals

- Wherever you are, learn about the habits of local animals so you can avoid them.
- Make plenty of noise when you are out walking; this keeps animals at a distance.
- Many animals are nocturnal. If possible, avoid being out at night.
- If you are collecting water from a place where animals drink, be alert.
- Always shake out your clothing and footwear before putting them on.
- Always wear shoes and keep your arms and legs covered.

Keeping insects out of boots!

When you take off your boots at night, cover the openings of each boot with a pair of socks. This prevents creatures from crawling inside.

Animal signs

Keep your eyes open for any animal signs, such as tracks, droppings, scratchings, and the remains of meals. With experience, these clues can tell you which animal left them, what it has been eating, and in which direction it is traveling.

A bear has a broad track with five toes and claws.

A jaguar has four toes; its claws are hidden.

Beware the mosquito!

Mosquitoes are a nuisance, and in some places spread disease. Sleep under a net and, unless you are in bear country, use plenty of insect repellent. If you are in a swarm, cover every part of your body and protect your head with a net or clothing. Check whether you need to take antimalarial medication before visiting different parts of the world.

IN THE wild you take more notice of the natural world. Following the movement of shadows on the ground helps you keep track of time. Noticing the clouds helps you predict the weather.

Making a sundial

Stand a stick in the ground. On a sunny day, mark the end of the stick's shadow early in the morning, at midday, when the sun is overhead and in the evening before it sets. Draw a semicircle between the first and last points (using another stick and a piece of string) and mark the midday point. This gives you a "dial" on which to measure time.

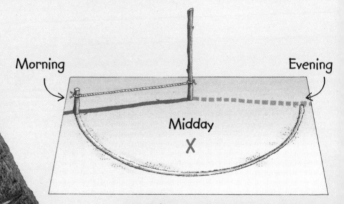

Morning

Evening

Midday
X

Cut lines
on a stick

Keeping track of the days

If you are lost or shipwrecked, it can be important to keep track of the days. You can do this easily by making a mark each morning on a rock, tree, or stick.

Predicting the weather

Predicting the weather helps you be well prepared.

- Learn to recognize changing cloud patterns. Clouds that bring rain are usually black, low, and massed in large groups. In dry weather, clouds are high, white, and fluffy.

- Notice the wind. A change of wind direction or strength may mean a change in the weather.

Closed   Open

- Watch for natural signs, such as pine cones. A pine cone closes when the weather is wet, and opens when it is dry.

Red sky in morning, sailor take warning. Red sky at night, a sailor's delight.

Keeping out the cold

If you are unexpectedly caught in very cold weather, stuff your clothes with moss or dry grass. This keeps warm air trapped inside and stops cold air from seeping in. It may feel uncomfortably scratchy, but it could save your life!

RESCUE is often the quickest way out of a dangerous situation. If you need help, try to get the attention of passing travelers. Thinking of ways to get help gives you less time to worry.

Keeping positive

A positive attitude is very important when you are lost in the wilderness. It can help you to combat fear, pain, hunger, and thirst. Stay alert and think about your surroundings. Try to find the key to survival. Keep yourself busy, and never give up.

Useful signaling methods

Signaling is a good way of attracting attention. Choose the best signaling method for your environment.

- A mirror or CD is good for signaling in bright sunlight.
- A whistle helps to alert searchers who are already in earshot.
- A flashlight moved from left to right makes an excellent signal.
- Signal fires that are quick to light and burn strong may attract a rescue plane.
- Flares are bright but do not last long. Use them only when rescuers are near.

Just a phone call away

If you survive a plane crash or any other disaster, look through the wreckage for any Cell phones or radios. You may be able to get help sooner than you think!

SOS!

In an emergency, you may need to send a "SOS" (Save Our Ship or Souls) signal. You can do this with a ground-to-air signal (try a message in sticks or stones). Make sure your message is big and that its shape and color contrasts with the land. Or try using Morse Code. In Morse code, the letter S is represented by three dots (short, quick signals), and the letter O by three dashes (long, slow signal). A radio, a whistle, puffs of smoke, or flashes of light are four ways of sending the signal.

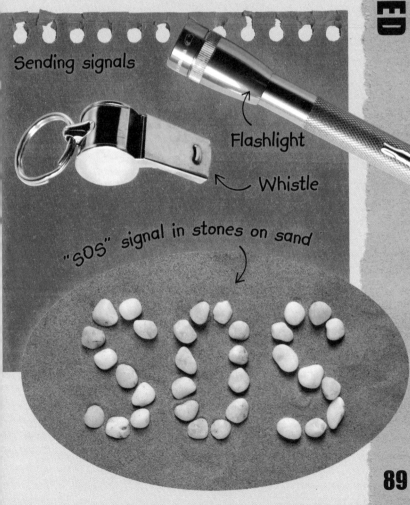

Sending signals

Flashlight

Whistle

"SOS" signal in stones on sand

WHEN you are lost, you have to decide whether to stay put or try to get out. It is usually best to stay where you are and wait until help arrives. If you do have to travel, be very careful.

Losing your way

If you lose your way, try to relax. Look at your compass. If you cannot find your way, stay put until you are rescued. Only set out if you are in real danger (for example, from flooding). Concentrate on finding shelter and leaving clues that will make finding you easier.

If you set out

Try to climb to a high point to examine the land around. This will help you choose the easiest route. Leave notes or signs for any rescuers, and mark your trail well. Do not rush as you move along; you will only get tired or injure yourself.
Set a slow, steady pace with plenty of rests.

Leave a trail

If you decide to travel, make sure someone could follow you. Tie clumps of grass into knots, leave arrows made of pebbles on the ground or in a real emergency mark tree trunks.

Experts cross rivers the safe way: by using ropes and special clips.

How to cross a river

- Rivers are dangerous. DO NOT try to cross one unless you are with a group.
- If there is a group of you, link your arms together with the biggest, strongest person upstream. Cross the river slowly and carefully.
- If there are three of you, form a huddle. The strongest person stands upstream and makes his or her way across the water. The others follow carefully.
- The safest method is with ropes and clips (karabiners) with a trained team.

PROFESSIONAL HELP may be far away when you are injured on a trip. First aid provides vital relief to stop bleeding, prevent infection, and can make a person more comfortable until medical help arrives.

First aid kit

Always pack a first aid kit when you go away. It should include pads, bandages, adhesive tape, antiseptic wipes and cream, scissors, and safety pins. Put everything in a waterproof container that will keep the contents clean and dry.

How to treat a burn

1. Put the burn in cold water for ten minutes.
2. Dry the area gently and protect it with a non-stick pad. Bandage it lightly, fastening the end with a safety pin.

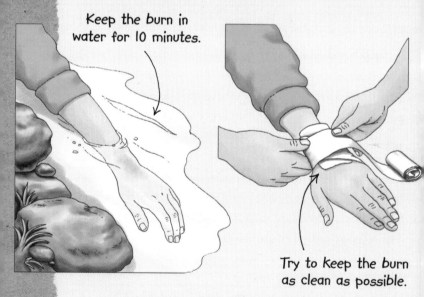

Keep the burn in water for 10 minutes.

Try to keep the burn as clean as possible.

How to treat a broken arm

1. It is very important to support the injured arm. Take a large triangular bandage or cloth, and slide it under the arm.

2. Bring one corner of the bandage around the back of the neck. Now bring a second corner up over the arm to meet it, and tie the two corners together at the shoulder.

3. Fold up the third corner of the bandage and pin it in place.

Triangular bandage

Secure knot at the shoulder

Third corner fastened in place

Blisters!

If you are walking and feel your feet getting sore, protect them right away with adhesive tape. This could prevent you from getting a blister.

ROPE and string are often used to fasten outdoor shelters, make fishing lines or even lifelines. Knowing how to tie good knots is a very useful skill.

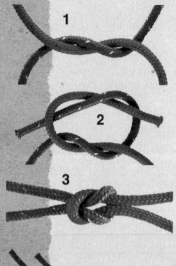

Square knot

A square knot is a strong knot that is easy to undo even when the rope is wet.

1. Cross the right piece of string over and under the left one.
2. Now take the left end and cross it over and under the right. Hold onto both ends.
3. Pull both ends to tighten the knot.

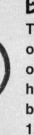

Bowline

This knot is used to make a loop— one that can go round your body on a lifeline, for example. Decide how big the final loop needs to be before you start on the knot.

1. To tie the knot, make a small loop over the rope and bring the end up through it from behind.
2. Now take the end around the main rope and bring it back down through the loop.
3. Pull the main rope and the end to tighten the knot. Now you have a loop that will not tighten or slip (though it could come loose).

Page numbers in **bold** show main references; *italic* refers to information given in picture captions.

The American Red Cross, a humanitarian organization led by volunteers, provide relief to victims of disasters and help people prevent, prepare for, and respond to emergencies.
American Red Cross
P O Box 37243
Washington, DC 20013
For an individual chapter in your state look on the website at
www.redcross.org

The Federal Emergency Management Agency or FEMA comes to the aide of natural disaster victims and their families.
Federal Emergency Management Agency (FEMA)
500 C Street, S.W.,
Washington, D.C. 20472
Phone: (202) 646-4600
Website address:
www.fema.gov

Boy Scouts of America
The purpose of the Boy Scouts of America is to provide an educational program for boys and young men to build character, to train in the responsibilities of participating citizenship, and to develop personal fitness.
Boy Scouts of America, National Council
P.O. Box 152079
Irving, Texas 75015-2079
www.bsa.scouting.org
For more information about Scouting in your area, please contact your local council.

Girl Scouts of the USA
Girl Scouts of the USA is an informal educational organization dedicated solely to girls, accepting and nurturing Girl Scout environments, encouraging girls in small groups to build character and skills for success in the real world.
Girl Scouts of the USA
420 5th Avenue
New York, New York 10018-2798
Phone: (800) GSUSA 4 U
www.gsusa.org

Hostelling International
Helping everyone, especially the young, gain a better understanding of the world and its people.
American Youth Hostels, Suite 840,
733 15th St N.W.,
Washington, DC 20005
Phone: 202-783-6161
Fax: 202-783-6171

American Rescue Team
The American Rescue Team International
P.O. Box 489
Alameda, CA 94501
Tel/Fax (510)523-5493
Email: amerrescue@aol.com

Outward Bound
If you're looking for ways to do more with your life, see more and be more, then you're ready for Outward Bound, leaders in wilderness challenge and adventure.
For more information and a catalog call: 1-888-882-6863

Acknowledgments

t=top; b=bottom; l=left; r=right

The Publisher would like to thank the following for permission to use their photographs:
5 www.osf.uk.com/Daniel J. Cox; 6 Still Pictures/Daniel Heuclin; 6/7 Digital Vision; 8/9 Digital Vision; 10/11 Digital Vision; 11 Ardea/Ron & Valerie Taylor; 12/13 Digital Vision; 14/15 Digital Stock; 16/17 Digital Vision; 17 www.osf.uk.com/Phil DeVries; 18/19 Marshall Editions; 20/21 Digital Vision; 22 Digital Vision; 23 FLPA/Steve McCutcheon; 24/25 Dave King; 26/27 Digital Vision; 28/29 Digital Vision; 30/31 Background Digital Vision; 30/31 MCSi; 32/33 Digital Vision 34 Andrew Sydenham; 34/35 gettyone Stone; 36/37 Background MCSi; 36/37 MCSi; 38/39 Background Digital Vision; 38/39 MCSi; 40/41 Background Digital Vision; 42/43 Dave King; 44/45 Digital Vision; 46/47 Ardea/Jean-Paul Ferrero; 48/49 MCSi; 50 Digital Vision; 51 Dave King; 52 Digital Vision; 53 Robert Harding Picture Library; 54/55 Digital Vision; 56 wwwosf.uk.com/Edward Parker; 58/59 Digital Vision; 60/61 Marshall Editions; 62/63 Digital Vision; 63 MCSi; 64/65 Digital Vision; 66 Digital Vision; 67 Mountain Camera/John Cleare; 68/69 MCSi; 71 MCSi; 72 Victorinox; 73 Corbis/Paul A. Souders; 74 www.osf.uk.com/ Colin Monteath; 75 Marshall Editions; 76 MCSi; 78 tl Ardea/D.Avon, tr Ardea/Peter Steyn, bl FLPA/Tony Wharton, br Bruce Coleman/Janos Jurka; 79 MCSi; 80 MCSi; 84 MCSi; 85 t FLPA/Mark Newman, b www.osf.uk.com/Michael Fogden; 86 MCSi; 87 Digital Vision; 89 MCSi; 91 Mountain Camera/John Cleare; 94 MCS.i. Thanks also to Craig Smillie and Orvis for loaning equipment. Illustrations: 70, 77, 81, 82/83, 86, 92/93 Peter Bull Art Studio and 87 Peter Sarson.